In My Sights

J. D. "Buck" Savage

In My Sights

Musings from One of America's Top Law Enforcement Trainers

Dave Smith
aka J.D. "Buck" Savage

To order additional copies of this book, contact:
Xlibris Corporation
1-888-795-4274
www.Xlibris.com
Orders@Xlibris.com
49344

CONTENTS

Dedication

To all the Heroes whose names honor the Wall, we will never forget.

PREFACE

When David Griffith, the editor of **Police**, approached me a few years ago and asked me if I wanted to write for the magazine's back page, I was thrilled. Then he told me what they paid . . . "it' the last page for Pete's sake," he argued, "why would we pay very much for that?" Hard to argue with that so I agreed, figuring I would run out of ideas in a few months anyway.

Incredibly, I am still writing these little essays of my life and thoughts, and still driving the staff at Police magazine crazy with my cute little way of turning them in at the last possible moment while still giving poor Sequoia Blankenship time to create one of his brilliant illustrations.

My wife, the Sarge, has graciously allowed me to keep the pittance I am paid as my "gun fund" so it has led to a string of firearms coming in over years that I absolutely, positively, couldn't live without! For that I am truly grateful.

Also, I must also apologize to all my amigos over the years that I've specifically mentioned in my articles, much to their chagrin. These little missives are based on "my" memories of what happened and if you remember it differently you are probably close to the same age I am and just as confused. Just send me your corrections in an email because those are a lot easier to lose than a letter.

It has always been my hope that the reader will find these articles entertaining and at the same time, a good reminder of tactics, ideas, and values that are an integral part of the mindset of a good crime fighter. Law enforcement is truly one of the heroes paths and it has been my honor and my joy to have been involved in it and with the men and women of it all my adult life (being a man, I consider adulthood an "age not maturity" thing).

Finally, to all my crime fighting friends over the years that I haven't written about yet, keep worrying, I am not yet done writing . . .

Dave Smith March 9, 2010

ACKNOWLEDGMENTS

As with any book the author always wants all the credit, but like most good things in our lives there are others who have added so much. First, I want to thank the great folks at *Police* magazine who talked me into writing about, well, me: Leslie Pfeiffer Maris, David Griffith, the always gracious Melanie Basich, who has a wonderful way of scolding me into doing my assignment; and, of course, Sequoia Blankenship, our quick-witted illustrator .

Then, of course, "The Sergeant," Betsy Brantner Smith, who is always happy to change my odd, stream of consciousness writings into coherent sentences. Her gentle way of pointing out my mistakes has, on several occasions, left me feeling like a rookie in charge of a homicide scene, but her moral support always brings me through.

My friend and neighbor, Tony Dawson, not only drops everything to help with edits, but also is my sounding board to make sure my point has been made along with my humor; two elements essential to these essays.

And finally, I have to thank all the wonderful men, women, and dogs that have made law enforcement the great adventure it has been for me. It is an ever growing list of folks who make us laugh, sometimes make us cry, always inspire, and are the reason we are a free people.

THE PATH

Warriors of all kinds soon
learn that the battle goes not to the swift
and the talented, but the determined.

I went to a youth swim meet recently. The viewing gallery in the natatorium was jammed with several hundred alternately thrilled then bored parents and friends of the competitors. Time moves so slowly at a swim meet, until the kid you're there to watch swims, that you can actually feel yourself aging.

I was sitting there trying to age gracefully when I noticed a girl in a wheelchair moving up to the edge of the pool as her race was getting ready to start. Since she was paralyzed from the waist down she could not start with a great leap into the water. So she lowered herself into the pool and pushed off with her arms. I wondered if her parents were worried about her being embarrassed by having to compete against kids whose legs didn't act as two great anchors, but instead provided a large part of the thrust to carry them through the water.

She lost the sprint by a wide margin and received a smattering of applause for finishing, but now she was getting ready for a much longer race and the stroke was the breaststroke. I tried not to stare as the girl lowered herself without aid into the water and the race began. Don't stare and embarrass her, I thought, and resumed my conversation with the parents around me.

As I sat there talking, I noticed the swimmers with working legs had just finished as our little swimmer with the useless legs was just coming to the last turn. She was far behind, but still she was determined to finish.

Then I saw the next race was being set and the swimmers were taking their marks. The Starter thought everyone had finished and was about to fire the pistol. I was on my feet, shouting, pointing at the little girl pumping so mightily, so far without legs that kick, lungs burning, arms aching, forging on in spite of the pain. Then there were many of us standing screaming, "Wait!" and the Starter lowered his pistol and turned to look at our girl.

We began to cheer in one great roar. We were with her now; we could not look away anymore for we had stood as one to demand she be allowed to finish. Now we had to acknowledge what we had known all along. We looked away from her as she lowered herself into the water so we would not have to wonder what her struggle might be, what her life might be like, how could she struggle so. Now, we knew: she was not racing the other kids, she was just racing life, making it come with her and follow her path. She was not following a path forced on her by life; she was just doing what she had done all her life, living well.

As she finished the race, she grabbed the edge of the pool gasping, turned to the crowd, and raised her goggles. She looked amazed at all the people standing and cheering; what was their problem? Once again, as she had earlier in the day, she refused a hand offered to her and boosted herself out of the pool and then awkwardly into her chair. Unlike earlier though, we did not look away; we stood a moment longer just watching her . . . amazed.

I firmly believe the world is full of cowards and thieves and idiots; it also has innocents and saints and heroes. I believe that we who wear a badge and a gun have chosen the warrior's path and that is one of the paths of the true hero.

We should celebrate that, and we should seek out those who choose other paths of the hero, for they are our brothers and sisters. That is why I had to write this to tell you something. I saw your little sister swim a race today . . . she was marvelous.

TAKING THE BITE

A disappointed K-9 has to sink its teeth into a target or
it will become complacent. What are you doing to stay
focused on the job?

I would later reflect on the odd incongruity of the K-9's toenails gently striking the tiles in the Junior High that we had just cleared. They were so dainty, almost tentative, as he rounded the corner into the shadows of the dead-end hallway where I hid silently in darkness. After that, he was a blur of snarling teeth and crushing power gripping my extended right arm.

I quickly began to understand that the veterans had, in fact, lied to me about how fun this was going to be, and that the honor of taking a bite from a disappointed K-9 that had searched the school and had suffered the frustration of finding nothing was actually a great time only for one of us, the monster German shepherd that bit me!

Now, I am a dog lover by nature, having grown up with at least one around me all the time. In fact, I currently live with three of them, including a shepherd who I have not and will not aggression train. She is our giant, almost 100-pound puppy, but there are moments, split seconds in time when we are playing rough and she gets that look. That look makes me think back to the instant I understood the truth about dogs: they still carry the complete DNA of the grey wolf and secretly, desperately, love to bite something.

If you have never participated in a K-9 Unit training session, know that it is one thing to watch a K-9 tear the pants off of a suspect and quite another to take the bite yourself.

Yeah, if all you've ever done is see the end result of all the training, then I invite you to go find a way to volunteer and learn at the deepest emotional level why dogs hooked up with us to begin with. They say over 100,000 years ago men and wolves started migrating and cooperating together on the hunting of migratory herds. Eventually wolves became dogs, so they could trick us into giving them the food at the end of day without them ever leaving the couch. But what they really want to do, desperately want to do, is bite something for us, especially another one of us.

I guess what is disturbing at a visceral gut level is that dogs don't care about uniforms or right or wrong. That is why the training of these land-sharks is so vital and at the same time has a few important reminders for us. K-9s are taught to absolutely comply with their handler's commands, so even though they love to bite they know they must let go finally upon command. Next, dogs are taught to be fearless . . . sadly, this is because they are expendable, and you are not!

Finally, it often struck me as odd that the reason I was in that school was so a disappointed dog could bite me and be happy. So the dog would not become detrained by routine and would go into every situation expecting to find someone . . . expecting to bite someone. Conversely, the city was perfectly happy to let me search a thousand schools, and shops, and businesses and find no one, regardless of whether it was training me to expect to find nothing or not.

The real lesson I learned from taking that bite was the true role of training as an antidote to routine and false alarms and compliant people, and how important it was to give our in-service officers a chance to get a bite. After all, we don't want them detrained any more than we want our K-9s detrained.

THE REAL FEAR FACTOR

Eating worms is not a display of courage. Going after
the bad guys is a display of courage.

Fear is a funny thing, not in the "ha-ha" way but in the "sheesh," eye-rolling way. It has been the focus of countless books, poems, and songs and has probably motivated more innovations than any other human emotion. Philosophers have argued that without fear we cannot have the virtue of courage; for courage is the Golden Mean between cowardice and recklessness, and fear is your guide.

Experts tell us that when we list our fears, we all have some pretty common ones. Remarkably, we rank fear of death between seventh and 12th, depending on who is writing the book.

Yeah, right. I call 15 yards for BS on that. I think those folks need to get sent to a "shots fired" call or "robbery in progress" call to experience some good old fashion pucker factor. "Pucker factor," great term. It figures it would be law enforcement language. We don't get afraid. We get a pucker.

Pucker makes us safer, faster, stronger, more tactically sound; it is our friend. It's amazing what it can do. I was jogging near my former home in Tucson and my right foot landed next to this odd looking tail with rattles attached. Pucker factor took over, I set the world long jump record. I swear my left foot came down near the Mexican border. What I would have given for some witnesses to that feat.

All of you have similar stories of remarkable feats you have performed under the influence of pucker factor. Recently my wife, "The Sergeant," was attacked by an emotionally disturbed bodybuilder who attempted to disarm her. Both ended up in the emergency room, but the dirtbag stayed. She used her pucker factor to turn herself into 118 pounds of really ruthless butt-kicking crimefighter.

The key to dealing with fear is not in avoiding it, but controlling it. In fact, we often get hurt when we ignore it. There should be a healthy amount of pucker factor whenever we get ready to search a building, make a traffic stop, cuff a subject.

It is the absence of pucker that often causes the careless and lackadaisical mistakes that injure and kill us all too frequently. So I think we should change lackadaisical to "lackapucker."

One antidote for lackapucker is to read the officer killed and injured summaries and then visualize what really happened and what it would have been like if you had been there.

This little exercise is also essential in controlling our pucker factor. When fear takes over, our performance drops like a rock, and the best way to control it is through training, both physically and mentally. If we have faith in our skills and abilities, we can use our pucker factor to make us stronger and faster and safer.

Finally, I am not a fan of all these reality shows on television and one that really gets my goat is "Fear Factor." I mean, come on, let's get some real fear going on this show, not some silly exercise in eating worms, holding one's breath under water, or high-altitude stunts in which the participants all wear safety gear. Let's see some pucker: take off those safety lines; chow down on something that you have to eat before it eats you. Heck, let's add some real intensity and send the "Fear Factor" contestants on a "man with a gun" call with you. That way they will know true pucker and see its greatest result: courage.

MAKE IT STICK

Officer safety lessons should be delivered in plain and
memorable language.

"Watch the Hands!"

—J.D. "Buck" Savage

The French have a saying; in fact, they are full of sayings, unfortunately none of them is pertinent right this second, but it makes the point that everyone has sayings. The French tend to have rather pithy ones, while the Irish tend to have warm ones. Sayings come in many forms and meanings and each of us finds ourselves drawn to the ones that carry the most meaning, or simply make us sound wiser than we are.

One of my favorites is: "Never wrestle with a pig; you both get dirty and the pig likes it." I like to use it from time to time to make the point that I am no longer interested in continuing an argument that I am losing. I will say this as I look away with a bemused expression that makes me appear bored and intelligent all at the same time.

Good sayings are easy to remember and make us better at what we do. They teach us life lessons or give us insights without the pain of experiencing them. I bet right now you can think of three or four sayings that allow you to remember to act, or even more important not act, a certain way.

While my face never did get "stuck that way," my grandmother's warning did change the faces I made. Recently, I was reading a book about ideas that "stick" with us. The authors explain the traits an idea should have for it to be easy to remember for a long time and help modify our behavior.

As a law enforcement trainer, I am always looking for ways to get my ideas across better. Over the years some have worked well, some haven't. Humor works well but it is also a good way to end up in sensitivity camp being reprogrammed. I have been to that woodshed a few times . . . Buck Savage was a great idea but not everybody thought it was funny and a few of those were high above me in the organizational chart.

Many folks come into a class or meeting not as participants, but as monitors, and humor is one of the trip wires of political correctness. But sayings are another thing. They tend to not push negative buttons but instead give us images that reinforce our points and allow them to be retained longer. I think we need more sayings in law enforcement.

Here is a good example: When I say "the 21-foot rule," crime fighters instantly recognize what it means. They probably saw it demonstrated in the academy, and they remember the safety message with just this simple saying. On the other hand, trainers often express their ideas in very smart sounding ways such as "a subject who is armed with an edged weapon and seven meters or closer to an officer with a holstered weapon will, in all probability, be able to successfully reach the officer prior to said officer drawing the holstered weapon and delivering two rounds." Sounds smart but it isn't very memorable.

Which is the goal! We need to make our training memorable; it needs to be "sticky!" In their book, "Made to Stick," Chip Heath and Dan Heath explain how our brains remember ideas and how we can make things easier to recall. One way is through memorable sayings.

A profession that faces so many risks needs to have lots of memorable lessons that mitigate those risks. I think we need to make up a bunch of sayings and plaster them all around. Things like "routine is what we are doing right before we get hurt," "bad guys' cars break down too," and "saw drunk, arrested same" have meaning for us that we can recall easily and help us stay safe, write reports better, and just generally do our jobs better.

So, the next time you are writing a general order, preparing an in-service class, or writing an academy lesson plan think about the core ideas you are trying to convey and make them stick when they hit the brains of the folks you are trying to change.

THE PLAN

Even in police work, no plan survives first contact
with the bad guys.

"Jump into the fray then decide."

—*Napoleon Bonaparte*

In the beginning we had a warrant and no plan . . . a void. We spoke among ourselves, "what would we do?" and then . . . suddenly he was there, the Sergeant. He stepped to the board, the marker flew into his hand, and suddenly there was The Plan . . . and he said, "It is good." We now had order in our minds, confidence in our hearts, diagrams on our clipboards, gas in our tanks, armor on our bodies, and we went forth righteously to execute The Plan.

I was one with The Plan and, being such, I stood at the door side by side with another as we knocked, announced to the answering felon, and made entry followed by our hearty cohorts as spoken in The Plan. Thus, I knocked and knocked and knocked as directed in The Plan . . . but no one came forth . . . no one shouted a greeting . . . no one seemed to move within . . . there was no answering felon . . . and then my backup left. I did not know why, but I knew that was not in The Plan.

Suddenly, the door flew open and there stood a man . . . a very large man . . . a bodybuilder. He was definitely NOT in The Plan. Still, I calmly announced my station and my mission, awaiting both my backups and a response from this fellow who resided in the house of illicit drugs who somehow, someway, had not been included in The Plan. Worse, he was not with The Plan . . . he was not of The Plan . . . he was of the Land of the Spontaneous, from which the fog of battle arises, the chaos of conflict evolves . . . for without speaking he smote me on the nose and fled.

But I had been one with The Plan! I was in The Plan, I was happy with The Plan, I was bleeding like mad . . . that was not in The Plan either . . . damn . . . so I abandoned The Plan. I roared and raced after my assailant through the house of drugs while villains sat about watching their television with far too much volume.

As I caught my Goliath, I screamed my commands and applied intermediate force upon his person . . . I seemed a madman and the other occupants sat terrified and frozen watching the carnage on the floor in front of their television . . . while not in The Plan this seemed to be working much better than The Plan itself.

Ah, and now my comrades, my amigos, my friends appeared . . . but not as highly disciplined warriors of The Plan . . . more like Vandals sacking Rome . . . bellowing, raging, searching with vengeance for they were enraged at the sight of my blood! O Chaos, what hast thou done to The Plan . . . for there was great clamor and shouts and commands and those who tried to flee were stopped short and those who tried to flush were left . . . flushless . . . and suddenly there was order . . . chaos had fled.

As we looked at one another, victorious in our conquest, we were suddenly . . . following The Plan. I was filling out our booking slips, another was listing the evidence and contraband being discovered, others were doing the discovering, and still others were interviewing those who did wrong and once again . . . we were with The Plan.

Finally, we looked about . . . at the drugs, at the prisoners, at the house, at my nose . . . and the sergeant said, "It is done." So ended The Plan, the good plan, a flexible plan, a plan based on a clear mission, a plan that stopped when humans do what they do, when chaos strikes, when accidents happen, or fate intervenes.

The wise sergeant said everyone needs a plan so they have something to abandon in a crisis . . . but, when our training and courage and initiative have overcome the threat, then we go back . . . back to The Plan.

A FUNNY THING HAPPENED ON THE WAY TO THE STATION

Sometimes you really do have to laugh to keep from crying.

It had been one of those long fruitless nights of surveillance and my partner and I were stuck in the gridlock of morning traffic trying to get to the station so we could get home and get some sleep. I was in the passenger side of the unmarked unit when I noticed a bicyclist go speeding by the stopped commuters.

We were in the inside lane and the fellow on the fancy road bike was flying along next to the curb, head down pedaling hard. "Maybe we should get bikes?" I said cynically as we watched the cyclist race past all the stopped vehicles.

Then a truck turned in front of him, and he went splat. "That's it, I'm sticking with cars," my partner said dryly and flicked his cigarette out the window as we slowly edged toward the accident and radioed for the paramedics.

All of you crime fighters have similar stories of macabre or ironic humor in the face of terrible events. In the book *Deep Survival*, Laurence Gonzales describes the way high-risk professions like fighter pilots, firefighters, and cops use humor to cope. It is a natural defense mechanism and seems to work well as long as innocent civilians don't happen to be standing within earshot when you make some wisecrack about really feeling like a burger right now as you pull a fast food bag out of a vehicle involved in a fatal wreck and hand it to a chuckling paramedic.

Often, the more tragic the event the more quickly humor injects itself into the scene. At the scene of a long undiscovered suicide my buddy J.W. surveyed the maggot hordes on the body and said, "I'm dying for Chinese right now!"

To the average civilian this would have seemed a pretty callous comment, but then the average citizen isn't closely inspecting a rotten corpse of a once beautiful woman who has taken her own life. And that same citizen isn't going to have to go into the front yard where a worried brother is waiting and give him a death notification and struggle to keep him from running into the residence to see an unimaginable sight.

The thing is, for J.W. and me it wasn't an unimaginable sight, but a very real horror that we needed to deal with. It was our job to deal with it, and that silly, callous little joke made the moment bearable, the task possible.

I have even joked and kidded with the dead themselves at scenes. Truthfully, I have done some of my best shtick talking to dead bodies. OK, they don't laugh, but they also never interrupt.

The real lesson in all this is that you need to keep that odd sense of humor. You will need it to make it through this wonderful profession. If you are a cop five years or more, you will have lived more life than the average citizen could ever know. But to cope with that experience, you will need to laugh.

Just remember, there are some things that are too terrible to laugh about. I will not talk about them here, but when such things happen around us or to us, the moment is often too tragic or too sacred to even joke about. In those moments, we just need each other, and it will be your caring, not your humor, that will make the difference.

Finally, in case you were worried, the bicyclist survived with only minor injuries. The paramedic turned to us as he was leaving and asked us for the story in detail. His response was, "Shame is, he would have been a hell of a donor." I answered, "Yep, in great shape and he doesn't smoke," then turned to look at my partner's cigarette firmly clenched in his teeth.

THE THRILL OF THE CHASE

There's something very primal and exhilarating about running after the bad guy.

I read the other day about an anthropologist who claims mankind's ancestors and modern canine's ancestors lived and hunted together more than 100,000 years ago. That might well be true. And as I look at the pack of people and dogs I call a family, I often wonder which species changed the other the most?

One of the most canine-like drives I have ever felt is the urge to chase, to pursue, to catch. I must confess to an odd primal thrill I always felt when a miscreant took off running. I wish I could say my mind thought "Tally ho!" in a thick British accent. But, alas, my inner thoughts were more like, "Fetch the bad guy. Fetch the bad guy . . . Yup, yup, I'm gonna fetch the bad guy!"

I could lie to you and say my foot pursuits were as graceful and swift as a greyhound, but I have a greyhound, and I run nothing like that . . . I am more in the category of say . . . a Basset hound. I am just as my high school football coach described me, "On the light side . . . but slow." This particular trait often caused my chases to go on for rather extended lengths.

Once, on the Navajo Reservation, I chased a misdemeanant for three miles! Even then, I was denied the joy of the catch since a Navajo DPS unit drove up to the guy as he came to a roadway and he just surrendered. All I ended up catching was a boot full of blisters. Officer Begay could not contain himself as he drove me back to my vehicle. Personally, I find giggling at another officer to be poor form.

It was on that same reservation near Chinle that I discovered the perfect medium for my poor running form and good endurance, deep mud. The Chinle Wash is a muddy riverbed the majority of the year and on the day in question almost no water flowed between its banks—only a vast ribbon of mud. I was tracking a bootlegger who had fled from a traffic stop and hidden in the tall reeds and trees that lined the wash when suddenly he bolted out from a bush in front of me and ran right into the wash.

I raced after him, landing in the mud and sinking six or more inches with each step. Thus began the most remarkable display of slow-motion running ever exhibited. Each foot could only be extracted with great effort and a resounding "plop" sound, and so it went. "Plop" . . . "Plop" . . . "Plop."

Gradually, it became apparent I was gaining on the lad! I would catch him within the hour. Realizing he was undone he turned toward the bank and aimed for a gap between two stout trees. Head down, he dove for the space . . . and missed. His head cracked into the tree on the left and he staggered back falling into the mud, trapped like a woolly mammoth in a tar pit. "Excelsior!" I cried. Not really, it just sounds more sophisticated than admitting I let out a great howl of joy at catching my prey.

Years later I still remember that as my favorite foot chase, and also concede what a great advantage I had over most officers in a foot pursuit. My quarry had nowhere to hide, and I could see his hands and what weapons, if any, they might hold. He had no corners to hide around, no cars to crawl under, no dark places to duck into.

So, the next time someone triggers your "gotta fetch 'em" gene remember this: there has been an increase in officers killed in foot pursuits over the last five years; so run wide around those corners, quick peek when necessary . . . and try to get them into the mud.

BACKING INTO SPACE

Sometimes the scariest scenarios provide the best training, and
show you what you're made of.

We took the elevator to the twelfth floor walked up two flights of steps to
a landing that opened onto an open rooftop overlooking downtown Los
Angeles. It was the middle of the night and the smiling LAPD SWAT officer
barely kept control of his giggle as he hooked my eight-ring to the rappelling
line and said, "Be sure to step quickly as you back over the edge." With
only the hookers and cabbies of downtown Los Angeles to bear witness, I
stepped backward into space 14 stories above the street.

That was 1982 and I still remember the sensations I felt as I stepped
back while looking into the face of Sgt. Ron McCarthy of the LAPD SWAT
Team. I was thrilled, scared, excited, and wondered how many times in
Arizona we would really ever get to make a rooftop assault from the top of
a 14-story building?

In fact, just a few days before, I had arrived at the LAPD SWAT School
as a member of the Arizona DPS SWAT and had never even rappelled before.
Yet now I was a veteran of helicopter rappels, building rappels, rappels where
I tied off and shot targets, and now I was in the midst of a training scenario
requiring a Spiderman-like trip from the top of a very tall building to a
window on the sixth floor.

The week I spent back then in sunny California was a truly eye-opening
example for me of how excellent training can produce remarkable results. I
was amazed at how well our instructors used positive modeling and aggressive
practice. We officers, deputies, and troopers from all over the country left
there not only better in our skills and tactics, but also with a great deal more
faith in ourselves.

With Sgt. McCarthy constantly walking around cajoling, teasing, and
laughing, the week was a whirlwind of exercises and tactics and camaraderie.

I had never, nor have ever since, experienced such a remarkable learning experience. LAPD was conducting the school to make money to buy equipment for the upcoming Olympic Games which would be held there, but the team members acted like we were joining their team and might be their backup someday. It was great . . . and scary.

The final training scenarios were designed to use all of the skills we had learned over the past week, and making us go almost an entire day straight was part of the stress applied to make sure we had the techniques down even while fatigued. The exercise that required me to rappel from such heights centered around freeing hostages on the sixth floor of a building in downtown L.A. The problem was you had to come from the roof to a window on the sixth floor.

Well, needless to say when the exercise was done and we sat around to debrief my heart was still pounding. Part of my brain was screaming, "Again! Again!" and another part was saying, "Are you outta your mind?"

Back then I had the "Skoal" habit and I was holding about two tins worth of dip in my lip as we went through the debrief. I was thinking about how the LAPD SWAT trainers had produced such incredible growth in so many folks in a week and I thought the keys were simple: they all led from the front, they expected a great deal from us and so they got it, and finally, whenever anyone had any problem whatsoever, the problem was the technique, not the person.

I took all these lessons back to Arizona and told my team about them. We never did a rooftop assault or even ever went to the top of a 14-story building just for fun, but the training changed the way I taught and what I believed about me. Thanks, Ron and the Team.

LISTEN TO YOUR LITTLE VOICE

Some people can give you great advice, but the best counsel comes from within.

"I owe my success to having listened respectfully to the very best advice, and then going away and doing the exact opposite."

—G.K. Chesterson

Whenever I try to explain what I have done for a living over the years, I always get to a point where the conversation slows down and I have to give a chunk of background and explanation. Why did I leave the Tucson PD if I loved it so much and go to the Arizona Department of Public Safety? Why did I take a job with a police television network and move to Dallas if I loved Arizona so much? Why did I . . . well you get the message.

In reflecting on these life-choices I have to say in retrospect I have had a darn good adventure of a life. The one thing I do remember is the abundance of advice I got before each of my decisions. Even the things that I thought were going to be well received and advice-free like doing the Buck Savage videos brought a lot of interesting advice from some pretty powerful people in my chain of command. I even had a Lt. Colonel advise me that I had better get a different uniform to do them in or my career would be rather stunted. That was some scary advice.

I think one of the hardest things in life is deciding what advice to take and what to ignore. I like to think most people give you advice they honestly think will be of help . . . OK I may be a little naïve, but I like to think that anyway.

The dictionary defines advice as "counsel or a suggestion as to a course of action," which also sounds a lot like the definition of training. In other words, what you should do in the future. The problem is that most people doing the advising don't have anything to lose if the advice is wrong. In fact, in many instances I have discovered the right thing for me turned out to be doing the very thing I was counseled against.

I was warned not to change departments. I was told not to select the Navajo Reservation for my Highway Patrol assignment as it was too remote. I was told a lot of things over the years that would have eliminated a great part of the highlights of my life if I had followed the suggestions given. Conversely, there were times when I was standing in minus temperatures with the wind whipping across the roadway arresting a DUI with my nearest backup two hours away if the highway stayed open and reflecting on the now wise warning given me on the day we were prioritizing our assignment wishes.

I guess that is the thing about advice and training . . . it all depends on how *you* use it. Ultimately, you need to be wise enough to know when and where to use the advice and when to ignore or even go against it.

As a fellow who makes a living giving advice to you, my brothers and sisters in law enforcement, I have to confess I am not going to be making your traffic stops for you or making a high-risk entry in your stead. I have done them and studied a great deal in order to give you advice, but you must always weigh such advice against what you know, what you can do, and where you are going to be doing it.

This holds true for all advice you get in life. I read a lot of articles by folks who make me wonder where they got the information or tactics they are writing about. Some seem wise and others foolish, but I challenge you to learn to listen to the one person you should absolutely listen to . . . yourself!

It is ignoring your conscience, your inner voice, that guarantees failure. When I have followed my inner voice, I have found great adventure and happiness. When I have ignored it, I have found myself later reflecting on what a fool I have been.

"PUT YOUR HELMET ON!"

Training in comfort when you work in the cold and hot is as
foolish as playing football
without protective headgear.

The other day I was on a wonderful modern indoor shooting range at a local PD. It is so convenient and comfortable, and it's equipped with the latest lighting options to recreate the various light conditions an officer may face on the street. As I was talking to the rangemaster, though, all I was thinking about was all the outdoor ranges I had qualified on, from the heat of Tucson to the frozen ground and howling winds of 21 degrees at Chinle on the Navajo Reservation.

That last one was quite an eye opener. We were in our heavy long johns, winter jumpsuits, and heavy coats; it was so hard to qualify. The hardest part was the fact that back then we carried our spare ammo in belt loops. The fake leather loops shrank so badly from the cold we could not get the damn bullets out without the greatest effort. Even our holsters shrank in the cold and our handguns couldn't be drawn unless we had belt keepers on, and even then our ability to clear leather quickly was diminished. As soon as we were done, I put a snubby in my right coat pocket and a speed loader in the left and that's how I patrolled in the cold from then on. The thing was, we would not have known of our equipment's limitations had we been shooting on an indoor range.

I thought about what I learned shooting in the cold way back when, as I watched the officers of the local PD leave their heated range where they trained in shirt sleeves. It was 21 degrees outside and getting colder. They put on their coats and hit the streets. Which made me wonder if any of them had actually trained in those coats.

One of the principles we "win" by is "practice the way you want to play." But one of the things we sometimes forget with our modern conveniences and comforts is that we want that practice to be as close to "game conditions" as possible.

I played center in football all through school, and the one thing I was really, really good at was long-snapping the ball back to the punter and holder. This is taken for granted by most fans, but it's not easy. The only way that you can get really good at it is through numerous repetitions. So I used to spend a lot of time in practice working on my long snap. Now, the long snap is hard in lineman's pads and at first I took my helmet off so I could look back between my legs better and snap my arms harder. The coach would race over every time he saw me do that and snarl "Smith, put that damn helmet on unless you plan to go into the game without it!"

The point is: when we do get the time to practice at the range and train for the street, we need to make sure we do them in "game conditions."

I asked the rangemaster of that local PD how they did their qualifying in the winter, and he said they not only made the officers wear their parkas but also their gloves when qualification time came along. I looked at the huge fellow, thought of my coach, and imagined him shouting "Smith, put on those damn gloves unless you plan on hitting the street without them!" I like that guy.

IN PRAISE OF CONDITION WHITE

When on duty, you need to stay alert and ready.
Off duty, your health depends
on some down time.

One of the basic concepts we have been using for decades now is Col. Jeff Cooper's "Color Code of Mental Awareness." I am sure you are familiar with this system, which says you should be in a condition of awareness of at least "Yellow" when on duty. Yellow could be described as a broad external awareness of the environment where you are processing whatever you see.

If you see a potential threat or something that requires greater attention, you should elevate to "Condition Orange." While in Orange, you are attending to the cues such as hands, vehicular movement, etc., that will require action. Ideally, your brain is focusing on the goal and not the skill at this time. If those cues trigger an action, you then go into "Condition Red," which is the execution mode.

Chuck Remsburg discovered when he was writing *The Tactical Edge: Surviving High-Risk Patrol,* that sport science had already done tons of research on mental and attentional patterns that make you a success in highly intense sports. These same skills make cops successful on the street.

In that book, the mental awareness pattern called "Condition White" took a pretty good slap. Condition White is the internal focus we go into all the time. In Condition White, you are not focused on the outside world. You do NOT want to have this mindset on the street.

But there are good things about Condition White.

Scientists tell us it is in this reflective mindset that we actually learn. When your brain is in Condition White, it consolidates whatever it has just learned, including motor skills. That's right . . . you don't actually improve while you are doing the repetitions but later when you are resting your brain.

Another form of internal focus is what we call "having a cobra in your face." When this happens, we are facing a real-life crisis and we are dealing with it internally . . . this is a bad one. It can constantly put us into Condition White while on patrol. So when we are having "issues" that predominate our thoughts, we need to make a concerted effort to decide we will deal with our "cobra" after our shift.

Yep, Condition White has a real important place in our life, but it ain't out on patrol. Now let's talk about off-duty. To be healthy, we must be able to have safe places to be in Condition White, and that is why I believe that you should teach your loved ones and off-duty associates how to alert you to threats, since off-duty you will be doing the things that make you healthy such as sitting around daydreaming.

I am a firm believer in teaching my loved ones "Secret Police Stuff." Actually, I just want them to pay attention to what the heck is going on around them . . . because sometimes I am in my favorite Condition White state . . . thinking about . . . well . . . nothing.

My wife, the Sergeant, asks, "What are you thinking?" when she observes me in Condition White. "Nothing," I used to say honestly, since I was truly in Condition White . . . peace. She never believed me and always demanded to know what I was "really" thinking, so I started to make up stuff. I guess women don't know the joy of Condition White. So, guys, let's keep this to ourselves and just make stuff up.

GOING THE WRONG WAY

Everybody makes mistakes; the important thing is
what you learn from them.

The really great thing about a career in law enforcement is all the exciting and wonderful experiences we get to have. Using Oscar Wilde's definition of "experience" as the name we give our mistakes, I have had a lot of "experiences."

Shortly after graduating from the academy, I was working mid-town on the graveyard shift doing my business checks when the "hot tone" went off and dispatch announced a 10-99—officer needs assistance, shots fired.

I screamed out of the alley heading to Speedway Boulevard with siren roaring. I knew that all I needed to do was get on Speedway, turn right, and I would be there in a minute. This I did without stopping at the stop sign and sliding very Hollywood-style sideways westbound onto the boulevard.

I can't express my surprise at seeing a parade of police cars screaming eastbound away from me. I had heard the street wrong. I was going the wrong way; I was never going to live this down . . . except . . . I had an idea! I took the first right and streaked around the block to join the parade going the right way within a few seconds.

Moments later a "Code Four," no further assistance needed, was broadcast, and the vast noisy parade of cars dispersed. I heard calls for Crime Scene Techs and a transport unit for a subject in custody, as well as an announcement that all officers were OK. What a relief. Our officers were OK and no one was the wiser about my mistake but me.

Next time I would get clarification; I would never do that again. I had been given a reprieve. I then began to inventory all the promises I had made to God if only we could keep this between us.

Then the voice of my sergeant came on my radio and commanded dispatch to have me meet him at the scene. Being a rookie, I suddenly had visions of a secret society of senior officers who secretly observed rookies, waiting for us to make big mistakes, with which they could mock us into insanity.

Such were my thoughts as I pulled up to the scene. The sergeant saw me arrive; walked toward me with an undercover officer I recognized as a legendary hard-ass. My God, they were going to double team me, I thought.

"Hey, Rookie, Joe is going to take you over to the scene with the Techs. He'll show you where the shooting went down and you get to diagram it while the Techs photograph it and gather the evidence."

I was undiscovered and I would learn about everything that went down right from the horse's mouth.

My list of prayed obligations had grown quite long by this time, and the rest of the night I would suddenly remember another one while meticulously drawing the best diagram I could of what had been a remarkable life-and-death struggle for one of my brothers.

As he took me through the alley where he had faced a gun in the darkness just minutes before, he expressed his disbelief that the suspect suddenly had a gun. He told me how he had leaped sideways and fired and friggin' missed, and what his pucker-factor had been. He talked to me of his mistakes in the moments of crisis, and I listened and expressed my admiration, and wondered what I would have done. He had done well. He had made mistakes, but he had never given up. He was human; albeit, a damn brave one.

He was also, however, never ever going to find out I went the wrong way when he was calling for help and chasing an armed rapist who had pulled a gun on him in an alleyway.

Take it from me . . . Some mistakes are best kept between you and your God.

A MASLOW MOMENT

*Bitching may be humanity's greatest need. It's certainly high on
the list for cops.*

Everyone has heard of old Abe Maslow. He is the creator of the "Hierarchy of
Needs," remember? The list starts with safety and ends with self-actualization,
which I think has something to do with eating our Wheaties.

Well, Maslow studied a lot of things and one of the things he determined
was this: If you see two patrol cars side by side, the officers are most likely
bitching about something . . . anything.

OK. Maslow didn't really say anything about law enforcement or even use
the word "bitching." What he said was, humans are the "Griping Species."
I'm not making that up. Maslow said it, and he was right.

We love to gripe, bitch, complain, whine, whatever you call it. It's as
human as breathing and like it or not we need to do it; we are going to do
it and, if we are honest about it, we enjoy it. The key, Maslow said, was
for organizations to find out where on the hierarchy of needs the need to
complain is. (See how he made it all about himself?)

That said, I need to do a little therapeutic whining, so here goes:

First of all, February deserves to be the shortest month, mostly as
punishment for Valentine's Day. What a mess that day is. No real parameters,
no real explanation except in grade school where they make you give everyone
a Valentine, even the kids you couldn't stand! Now, how did that prepare
us for life, or at the least, well . . . future Valentine's Days?! Mostly it's just
another great chance for us to disappoint the ones we truly love. One more
opportunity to forget, buy late, buy wrong, buy too big, too small, wrong
brand, too bright, and why? Who was Valentine anyway? Historians say it
could be three different guys . . . each did different things, so what are we
to do? I don't know! Who the heck decided we need to make Hallmark a
billion dollars?

All right, this is a book about law enforcement for law enforcement, so that's all I'm going to say about Valentine's Day. But it needed to be said.

Here are some other things that need to be said. And believe me, as cops, we're just the folks to do it. I believe we are the premiere gripers on this planet. I know I am, and I want to relieve a couple of other stress points I've got percolating inside:

- When is the truth about CSI going to come out? How many civilians truly believe the forensic techs taking the fingerprints at their burglary are going to be arresting the felon in 52 minutes?
- When are news-people going to learn that people get robbed and homes get burglarized and there really is a difference?
- Who the heck decided DNA is going to be at every crime scene? I am sick and tired of all these pseudo-expert talking-head goofs who show up over and over again on the news, making stupid statements about the "crime-of-the-week." If I hear the word "motive" one more time I am going to scream! Crimes have elements and motive is almost never one of them; guilt is determined by many forms of evidence and, even if a slimeball didn't leave any deoxyribonucleic acid at a crime scene, that doesn't mean he or she isn't a part of the deed!
- When is the public going to learn that on-video or not, winning a physical confrontation is going to look rough, kinda like Ultimate Fighting without the pay-per-view. A violent confrontation is never pretty and the public and the media need to be taught it ain't a "beating" just because the cop won! Use of force is ugly and eventually we need to educate the public to this. As cops, we have one rule . . . we win! And the community we protect needs to understand that.

There, I feel better. Dr. Maslow was right.

VOICES FROM ABOVE

A life of crime can be really confusing sometimes.

"All right. Come out with your hands up, two cups of coffee, an auto freshener that says 'Capricorn,' and something with coconut on it!"

—Chief Wiggum, *The Simpsons*

The thing about being a good burglar is that you have to know when to move and when to stay still. One of the really bad times to move is when a K-9 officer is using the pay phone in front of the building you are burgling.

It was a cold winter night in olden times when cell phones were only found in science fiction movies and on Dick Tracy's wrist. Back then when a law enforcement officer needed to make a call, he or she would give dispatch the number of the nearest pay phone and wait for it to ring.

The pay phone in front of the convenience store rang that night and the deputy who was returning home late from training with his furry partner answered and casually leaned against the phone staring off into space. Several moments later he noticed that the German Shepherd in the front seat of the patrol car was drooling and staring into the closed business. The deputy turned just as the burglar ducked behind the counter. Casually, the deputy advised the dispatcher to get the local crime fighters there ASAP as he had a burglary in progress.

Less than a mile away, my partner JW and I sat in an unmarked car watching some closed businesses on Speedway Boulevard. Tucson had been having a real rash of business burglaries, and we had been sent out in an unmarked unit so we could watch our business without giving our true identities away . . . Damn we felt covert! The hot tone and following burglary-in-progress code that went out put a thrill through the both of us and off we went with JW driving in his usual heart attack-inducing style.

With the dog and his partner securing the front of the store, we raced to the rear to block any escape. We found no point of entry; the back door was securely locked with no marks whatsoever. We then thought of the roof.

Since JW and I were so excited the veterans who arrived after us selflessly offered to let us climb onto the roof. Carefully, we worked our way onto the flat rooftop and saw the vent pried all the way back in the center of the building. With guns and flashlights drawn we peered down into the hole.

The perpetrator calmly stepped into our lights and looked up! "Get on the ground!" I screamed with great command presence and excitement.

"Keep your hands up!" roared JW with authority.

"Get on the ground!" I bellowed with great agitation and emotion. "Keep your hands up!" yelled JW with intensity from behind his flashlight and revolver.

"Get on the ground!" I yelled.

The thief was caught in mid-move, half crouched and his arms suspended about eye-level. We had brilliant lights blinding him while simultaneously giving him two very distinct commands. If he followed one, would the other one shoot him?

While we continued our very impressive display of command issuing and command presencing, the fellow decided to take his chances with the dog. He simply moved out of our sight, walked to the front of the store, unlocked the door, stepped out and got on his knees, and surrendered to the one cop there that could not give him confusing commands.

Today, JW is a chief and I make my living teaching such things as command presence. Um . . . so . . . we never speak of this event. But I like to think that somewhere there is a former felon who speaks to groups of young people on why they should not become criminals and about the night he heard voices from above that changed his life.

THE SEARCH

It was a dark and stormy night in Tucson and suddenly
a call came out for a burglary in progress.

Not long ago a good friend of mine was killed in an accident. He had gone
to the academy with me, been my roommate, and later worked the beat
next to mine for two years. We had the bond of on and off-duty friendship
and adventures.

In thinking of Sam I remembered the scariest building search I ever did.
It was a dark and stormy night in Tucson and suddenly a call came out for
a burglary in progress in Sam's beat.

A local doctor's daughter had taken the opportunity of her parents' trip
out of town to have a male friend do a sleepover. Suddenly, the back door
of the home was heard to open and the sounds of footsteps were heard
coming down the hall. Calling 911, the couple fled into the night to meet
the responding units.

I took the alley and saw that indeed the back door stood open. Sgt. Tripp
ordered Sam and me to make entry at that point while the perimeter of the
house was secured by veterans. The Sarge was always great about letting the
kids have all the fun.

With a pucker factor in the nineties, Sam and I entered and began our
methodical search for the home-invading miscreant. I remember thinking
how lucky I was that Sam was my teammate while we worked our way
through the large home. Halfway through the house, we got to the front
door and the Sergeant entered. We had a long hallway with two bathrooms
and three bedrooms left. It formed a kinda horseshoe and Sam was sent to
anchor the end and the Sarge turned to me and said, "Smith, clear the rest
of the house."

So I went, gun in hand, slicing the pie and quick-peeking my way from
room to room, as the anxiety grew and options for the perp to hide were

eliminated one by one. By the time I got to the last room, I could hear my own heart pounding. The bedroom opened at the other end into the space covered by Sam and no one had tried to pass. Slicing the pie again, I saw nothing and I moved quickly to the closet. Why do big houses have so many damn closets! Positioning my gun to cover any threat I quietly turned the handle and swung the door open . . . . there stood a shadowy figure.

To this day, I still wonder what that doctor was doing with a storefront mannequin in a spare bedroom closet. Startled, I took a step back but, miraculously, I did not fire my weapon, and I did not have a heart attack.

Then the neighbor's dog sprang from under the bed behind me! He had no doubt been terrorized by all of these cops in the house, and he raced into the sights of Sam, who further terrorized him by cursing in his unique way.

The incident over, the veterans laughed as they filed by the mannequin and saw the two wide-eyed rookies telling the sergeant we didn't know why we missed the muddy paw prints coming into the kitchen through the back door. Leaving, the Sergeant simply turned to us and said, "It takes as much courage to search an empty house as it does with someone hiding in it, when you don't know which it is!" He was a good leader, Sgt. Tripp.

I will miss Sam. Our shared adventures are bright points in my life. Our mistakes and successes were many, each of them leading us to grow and be better cops. Appreciate your "Sams." They are gone much too soon.

PERFIDY THY NAME IS FITNESS

*A man's got to know his limitations but still never give in to
being a couch potato.*

I love being in shape. Running an eight-minute mile, benching 300, riding a mountain bike on rugged trails, playing a rousing game of three-on-three, are all things I would love to be doing. But I can't do any of them today.

Yeah, I am a firm believer in fitness; it just doesn't seem too crazy about me.

In fact, I am currently typing this little essay with one hand and wondering what my next fitness fad should be? In the '70s and '80s I was quite the runner, doing everything from 5Ks to a marathon. Finally, an orthopedist pronounced my knees shot and that my running days were over.

So I got into lifting. I saw my lifts go higher and higher even as my age did too. It turns out strength stays with us well into our higher years, but with a catch . . . you have to keep at it. You can't store exercise and exercise is the only way to create fitness.

Maintaining fitness is tougher than raising fish. You have to keep feeding it and, if you feed it too much, it dies. Well, it doesn't actually die; it kicks back, like a mule.

The other day I was just doing my usual chest workout and was fully warmed up . . . I was toasty I was so warm and then "SNAP!" There was pain so severe I was in shock in two minutes . . . sweating, trying not to faint, the whole enchilada. I had pulled my left pec off my arm and had a weird lump on my chest.

So here I am, all trussed up, having gone through a three-hour surgery and planning what to do next to stay in shape. Yes, I get it; 53-year-olds shouldn't be doing one-repetition maximums with more than 300 pounds.

Lesson learned. But I'm not going to let it stop me. I have spent my entire adult life trying to maintain my body with masochistic activity. My first training position was as a fitness and officer survival trainer, and it is one of my deepest beliefs that we must always train our minds and bodies.

If we train right, we achieve that state we like to call fitness, a state of well-being that seems so darn hard to maintain with our lifestyle. Fitness is so selfish; it demands time, effort, patience, and balance . . . little of which we seem to have.

So we cut corners. We try to work out a bunch today so when we miss the next two workouts we won't lose anything. Then we injure ourselves. But we keep coming back . . . we have to.

I challenge you to find the things in life you can do to maintain your level of fitness, the things that match the most important things about you. First, find what fits your body type. If you look in the mirror and see a linebacker, don't train like a running back. All you are going to do is find yourself hurt.

Second, accept that time is against us all . . . we are going to age (if we stay lucky), and we need to adjust our routines to match these limitations. The real key here is to be sensitive to your physical changes and just work around them. I am not going to stop lifting but I am not doing maxes anymore and in just a few minutes I am going for a walk . . . yep, a wimpy old walk. Why? Because I must feed that burning need called "fitness."

GENERATION WHAT?

*You can't sum up the performance of recruits by the era in
which they were born and raised.*

OK, I confess. I used to teach how to train the "new generation." You older
cops know who I'm talking about: frankly, the generation not as good as
ours.

Well, I kept studying and studying because something kept bugging me
about all this research that was giving me this insight into the minds of the
different generations and the various things that made them tick. For one
thing, one of those generations was mine. Most of this theory was kicked
off years ago in a book curiously enough called *Generations* by William
Strauss and Neil Howe.

These two fellows have made quite an industry of this business of each
generation having a start date and ending date and what they are like, how
they work (or don't), and their various sins and virtues. Most administrators,
trainers, and many academics have embraced this whole thing as a touchstone
or crystal ball to solve the problems of the current workforce, or cadet class,
that just doesn't seem as good as "us." This was all well and good until Strauss
and Howe wrote *The Fourth Turning*. Or better yet, it was all well and good
with me until I read it. I now think it is high time we rethink this whole
generations-have-personality malarkey.

I think we should reject the whole enchilada and say simply that people
will grow up to be individuals . . . some good, some bad, some lazy, and some
just like you, dear reader, however you perceive yourself to be. One of the
things I noticed in my research about the various generations was that the
different traits each one had could be applied to anybody in the others.

For example, a generation could be described as "heroic and
self-sacrificing;" the GI Generation that saved the world in World War
II and created my remarkable generation known as Boomers is one such

group. But these marvelous folks still had their lazy, cowardly, materialistic, self-serving brethren, as it turns out all generations have. And in reality, in spite of the images presented by the modern media, few of my generation were at Woodstock, were hippies, marched on Washington, or went to Canada . . . I mean, who do you think actually fought (and sometimes died) in the Vietnam War?

I did notice recruits changing during the '80s, but who would think it was because a new generation was coming into its own? We still had good cadets and bad cadets, courageous cadets and scared cadets, smart ones and not so smart ones . . . I can read the same traits in Homer's "Iliad," describing a generation thousands of years dead. I think the important thing is not the student but the teacher, not the recruit but the instructor, not the worker but the leader who sets the standard and the expectations.

All this generational stuff is just speculation, no hard science; Strauss and Howe aren't even sociologists. Besides, if they are right, the newest group of recruits, the Millennials, are going to be just like the GI Generation because societies recycle generations every fourth one or so. Which means these kids get all the glory and we Boomers will forever be . . . well . . . spoiled brats. Well, I am not going to stand for that. All together now, (you Gen X'ers pay attention) "there is no such thing as generations having traits."

EMBRACING MY SINISTER SIDE

Regardless of your naturally dominant side, make sure you can shoot with either hand.

Being a "southpaw" is one of those things you don't quite understand until you start school. When I was little, people thought it cute I used the "wrong" hand with my crayons, but my teachers were frustrated that I never could adapt to writing with my right hand.

That was the '50s, when schools were still trying to convert left-handed people into right-handed ones, and I was one of their true failures. To my second-grade teacher I seemed like a bizarre alien child with strange powers of inability, since I did lots of things with my right hand but wrote with my left. She would constantly ask me what my problem was.

My problem was I was cross-dominant, an odd brain condition where I did power movement with my right side and all my fine motor skills on the left. I had all the classic symptoms such as difficulty learning to read, very poor handwriting, and a biting wit. Actually, the wit part isn't a symptom of cross-dominance but it sounds good. I have often thought it was the difficulties I had learning certain tasks that made me so curious about learning and performance, and helped make me a pretty good coach and trainer.

As I grew older I got better and better at just using the best hand for whichever skill I was learning, and thought it kinda cool that I used both hands; but my heart was still with the lefties. I'll never forget my high school English teacher, thinking herself quite clever, asking the class why I was sinister. Sinister? Me? Mr. Class Clown?

OK, fine, sinister also means on the left side, a term used in conjunction with us lefties; ah, but she didn't call the righties "dexter," even though dexter means on the right. Anyway, I did fine in English without further trauma and eventually found myself in the Academy.

While I used my right hand to strike, swing a bat, and shoot a rifle, I could shoot a pistol with either hand and had to pick a side . . . literally. Since my dominant shooting eye was on my right, I chose the right. I did find it amusing to watch others trying to shoot with their non-dominant side, since I had spent a lifetime changing hands while normal Southpaws and Righties had spent their lives neglecting their sad hand on the other side of the brain.

Then came the day I was looking into the eyes of mostly right-handed cadets and realized I had to get these folks to learn to shoot effectively with the other side of their body. I remembered when I had broken a finger in my left hand and had to write for the next few weeks with my right one. Good Lord was that frustrating! Even with my left hand my handwriting was terrible, but with my right it was not only nearly impossible to read but painstakingly slow to do as well. It was only with constant repetition that my right hand eventually wrote without me having to think about every letter, and actually became more legible than my left.

So I made the cadets do repetition after repetition until they learned to use both hands to shoot just as I had learned to write, and their scores soared. I only hoped they kept those skills up better than I did my right-handed writing skills; they went into immediate atrophy after my finger healed. The important thing for you is to make sure you can do your lifesaving skills with both hands . . . become cross-dominant on everything related to your firearms.

Learn to aim, fire, and reload your firearms with either hand and without having to think about every little step. It takes repetitions. How many it will take you will depend on many variables, but it doesn't matter; just do them! I know those of you who are cross-dominant will find this repetition boring, but we need to practice too. Dexter, sinister, or a combination, the world challenges us all . . . but I would like to gripe for a second about scissors . . .

CLIMATE CONTROL

*Mail carriers have nothing on cops when
it comes to working in
sleet and rain and blinding heat.*

I was going through the owner's manual on my truck the other day and noted the section titled "Climate Controls," and it reminded me of another difference between crime fighters and the folks we protect. Not only do we run to the sound of the gunfire while others run away, but we have to get out of our damn cars no matter what the weather. One of the first calls in my career was traffic control at one of the busiest intersections in the city with the temperature hanging at 110 degrees.

This isn't something you'll see covered in any department's recruiting pamphlet. How would it sell people on the job if it described the working conditions as: "Wearing lots of equipment, body armor, and a hat in blistering heat (or horrible cold) while generally risking your life." Doesn't sound like a great opportunity, does it? Oddly, it is.

Our profession is a great adventure. And part of that "adventure" is doing the job in the midst of a thunderstorm, or snowstorm, or windstorm, or whatever Mother Nature chooses for you to face that day. Nothing adds to the pucker factor like a nice little electrical storm while you're searching down an alley for an armed robbery suspect and cursing the K-9 units for being away at training . . . again.

Many of you work in areas that afford you the great opportunity to suffer a quick case of heat exhaustion in the summer and frostbite in the winter. Some of you have raced to a hurricane tragedy, a tornado aftermath, or a sudden flood. You know the thrill of the risk that rushes through you as you pull up to the scene and reach for your door handle. Often you will look around and see other citizens sitting in their cars or looking out the windows of their houses; they won't help the victims; they will stay where they are. But regardless of the conditions, you must get out . . . you must help.

Have you ever looked over at the "climate control" section of your dashboard and wished it could change the maelstrom you are about to jump out into? Regardless, you climb out of the cool (or warm), safe vehicle and step into the experience Ma Nature has waiting for you. Heck, the closest I ever came to drowning was in an Arizona monsoon, when I reached down onto the floorboard of a vehicle involved in an injury accident and a city bus drove by creating a wave that I could have surfed if I had a board.

I was lying on the seat reaching under the steering wheel to recover the victim's purse when the wave hit. I had my mouth open. One of Murphy's Laws for Police Work is: your mouth will always be open at the worst possible moment.

I crawled out into the downpour coughing and choking and carrying a purse filled with nasty water, similar to the water I had just cleared from my lungs. Needless to say, the accident victim didn't understand the Poseidon-like adventure I had just experienced and was just mad about her wet purse.

I know each of you has your own "storm story," your own weather adventure. I wish you well in the ones you will face in the future, and hope for a day when the folks watching you do your job appreciate the fact that you step into the real world so they can stay in their climate-controlled one.

THE CUISINE OF THE ROAD

Cops might not always eat the best food on duty, but every
meal tastes better when it could be your last.

Police work makes for some strange mealtimes and odd food choices. Having
worked all over Arizona, I can say I have eaten some of the best and some of
the worst meals of my life while on duty. Crime fighters who regularly read
MY column know I spent my formative years fighting crime in Tucson, but
I have failed to mention the change in my physical dimensions my rookie
year.

My beat only had three places to eat on graveyards. One was a fast
food joint where you ordered by speaking into a kid's toy. The two other
establishments gladly gave you a cup of grease on the side if you wished.
To say I supersized may be a slight overstatement, but it was the accidental
viewing of my new body as I walked by a mirror in the locker room that
started me running. Who was that chubby guy walking around with my face?
The next week I started running and didn't stop for the next 25 years.

Law enforcement officers tend to die younger than their civilian
counterparts, and one of the reasons has to be our diets. I did a stint as
a vegetarian on the Reservation when I was training for a marathon and
soon found myself fantasizing about burgers, fries, and grease on the side. I
discovered real Navajo tacos then and still remember thinking as I walked
out of a restaurant in Kayenta that I had just had one of the best meals I
would ever eat. Of course, we were heading out to the all tribal rodeo and
the odds of someone getting hurt were pretty high, so it was good to take
a moment and enjoy gastronomical delight.

I don't think it is an accident a cop often knows the best places to
eat. There is something about the nature of risk that heightens all of our
senses, and good food doesn't just nourish the body; it nurtures the spirit.
In narcotics we had our favorite Mexican and Japanese restaurants and I

remember sitting with my gang eating chorizo con huevos and thinking that **THE** warrant we were about to serve was only going to be made better by the afterburn of a good jalapeño.

I once did expert witness work in Nova Scotia and must say that the Maritimes leave their New England cousins behind when it comes to the creative ways a lobster will end up. The same is true for what Louisianans turn shrimp, crawfish, corn, and potatoes into. I have sat at a long picnic table in Baton Rouge after a day of the Torch Run eating food so spicy you sweat like you're still running and beer so cold you . . . **D**arn, I'm drooling.

Anyway, my point is this: **I**f you want a really good meal wherever you go, follow the local crime fighters. Somewhere in our brains is a junction of sensation and risk (my personal theory), a phenomenon that makes us truly appreciate a good repast. The fact that each meal may be our last is even more real for us than the average citizens going blithely about their day; **THIS MAKES THE MEAL** just a little more tasty, a little more satisfying than it might normally be.

It reminds me of an old Buddhist story of a monk who plucks a strawberry from the side of a cliff just before his vine is cut and he falls to certain death below and he thinks, "This is the best strawberry I have tasted!" And like the monk, we tend to eat fast since we are sure a call is waiting or someone needs us somewhere, but we still get the satisfaction of the food. This in no way denies the truth that some of my worst meals have been on the job as well, but the unique sensations a good meal gives those who truly live in the fast lane of life are intensified.

I don't go "on duty" anymore; I go all over the country training and speaking and make a point of asking the warriors that attend my classes where to eat in their area. They are always dead on. From tortas in Yakima to lasagna in Cleveland, my memories are filled not only with my great friends but also with great meals. Ah, too bad I had to give up running . . .

BACKING UP IS HARD TO DO

In and out of your car, shifting into reverse and
asking for help are critical survival skills.

Ask risk managers to tell you what causes the majority of vehicular accidents, and they will all sing the same tune: "Backing Up Is Hard To Do."

In fact, reversing accidents cost millions of dollars a year and many private companies go to great lengths to prevent them. One major parcel carrier will not allow its drivers to back up . . . period. This won't work for crime fighters, but knowing that putting your car in "R" can be one dangerous activity is the first step in making yourself safer.

We can all agree we need to back our vehicles up from time to time and do it safely, but what about ourselves when we are not in our units?

I was told in the academy that we were to never back down and never call for backup unless it was absolutely necessary. The guy teaching us this oozed machismo. Damn! He talked tough . . . and to a bunch of twenty-somethings that didn't know Scotch tape from crime scene tape, he was the law.

He was also totally wrong. I don't know if you were taught these old manly axioms in your academy, but I hope you had the good fortune to have a grizzled old curmudgeon working the same beat as you and that you started telling him all the stuff you learned in the academy about never backing up and only calling for backup when you were absolutely sure you needed it. That's what I did.

This veteran cop transfixed me with the special look he saved for dirtbags and growled, "Listen, Smith, you snot-nosed rookie, you are not being paid to take an ass-whipping, get shot, stabbed, or get me hurt by your being a dumbass! God gave you a pucker-factor for a reason. And when it gets high enough, it is time to get your rear-end outta there and get some backup. Something seems hinky, smells wrong, looks weird, you call for backup . . . period."

Now, let me put this into context. This guy was one fantastic beat cop who started his career in St. Louis and then came to Tucson because he heard it had a higher crime rate. He was a cop's cop, and I truly believe this brief moment of on-the-job training that he gave me to cancel out the macho tripe I was taught in the academy probably saved my life. I know for certain that it spared me a lot of ass-whippings.

Since my rookie days, I have studied officer safety and survival for decades, and I have found that the veteran's advice was sound and wise. We do have a wonderful capacity to sense when things are wrong and it is then we should call for backup . . . if we wait until we are absolutely certain we need it, it may be too late.

I wish I could tell you I have always followed that crusty old veteran's advice, but the other factor I have seen in myself and many others is the simple truth that backing up is hard to do. We have our pride at stake, and there have been times I stood and faced a group down when I should have walked away and gotten the backup I needed. All I can say is that sometimes we do have an angel on our shoulder because I should have gotten several serious beatings.

Don't count on angels or luck. Remember to back up safely in your vehicle, back up when your pucker—factor gets too high, and call for backup when you sense you might need it. When you fully understand what is at stake, backing up is not so hard to do.

DRESS FOR SUCCESS

A badly designed uniform can be a hazard on the job.

"Clothes make the man. Naked people have little or no influence on society."

—*Mark Twain*

One of our family friends came over the other day. I don't know when he joined a gang, but his baggy pants, cool bling, and baseball hat turned to one side caught me by surprise. "Whad-up?" he said, and I wondered what indeed was up with this well-raised son of hard-working parents?

Yeah, I know, times and fashion change. I actually wore leisure suits way back when. Yep, the '70s was a time of cool fashion. Cool even when it came to my first police uniform.

Tucson Police Department had a classy but oddly untactical uniform. We had blue wool pants, always in fashion in the Sonoran Desert, and a white shirt. Yep, white. Add to that shiny things such as nametags and badges and brass snaps and a really, really shiny badge dead center on the front of our mandatory, though blue, caps, and we were really visible to the bad guys.

Once, my amigo Sam and I responded to a silent alarm at an office center. When I carefully pulled on the door, much to my surprise it swung open!

Since the K-9 units were in training, we made our crossover into the building. There is a certain rush one feels entering through the "fatal funnel" of a doorway, especially as the number two person. Over and over in my head I heard our survival trainer saying, "They always get the second guy if they are going to shoot!"

Once inside, we carefully deployed our flashlights, turning them on to search the blackness. Soon, I began to notice when my light was off and I was moving that I could clearly see the ghost-lit upper torso of my partner.

Damn, I wondered if we should have popped a flashbulb first to blind the dirtbag who might have waited inside.

Once we cleared the call, we griped about the way we glowed in the damn dark. So we got with JW and Charlie and Morty and decided to alter our uniforms. We were certain we could get away with it since we were on permanent midnights and, besides, if they caught us, what were they going to do? Put us on permanent graveyards?

We all bought Navy watch caps and took our badges off our Ike jackets, which we would then put on before doing any high-risk activity. We had ninja'd ourselves up! This went great for several weeks until the watch commander arrived at a scene unannounced.

Sgt. Monk took most of the heat since he had allowed us to desecrate the Tucson PD's brilliant (in many ways) uniform and we went back to our traditional high-risk uniforms, careers intact but egos bruised.

Over my many years, I have seen some great and some bad uniforms from the tactical standpoint. I like formal uniforms for formal occasions and believe a well-dressed person can make a difference.

When that difference is catching a felon bent on wrongdoing, I think we need to make sure our uniforms are tactically sound. And speaking of sound, put on your uniform and jump up and down. How much noise do you make?

I can't tell you to change your uniform on your own as a crazy bunch of crime fighters did back in '75, but you can become your agency's champion for safe uniforms. There are times that you want to be seen and times that you don't. Your uniform should give you that flexibility.

MY LIFE AS AN EXPERT

If you ever want to know about the weirdest cases out there,
just serve as an expert witness in court.

One of the most stressful things I have ever done in my life is be an expert witness. Despite training hundreds of cadets at the academy, studying various law enforcement skills, developing hundreds of diverse training programs, as well as simply doing and supervising law enforcement in the true laboratory of the street, nothing prepared me for the surreal world of the expert witness.

My first case as an expert was defending a group of officers who had shot a naked fellow on a narcotics raid. He had sued and won and now the officers were appealing. Nakedness is an odd attribute for a suspect, but after working narcotics for years I found it is not that rare. In reading all the depositions I noted the officers and the experts seemed to live in two separate worlds.

To the experts, this naked fellow was shot rather excessively at close range by the officers even after he had raised his legs in surrender . . . that's right, his legs. On the other hand, the officers doing the shooting seemed to be rather unmindful of the fellow's nakedness or foot position; it was the presence of the rifle that he was swinging toward them that they found rather offensive.

I have found this paradox often in the cases I have worked. What seems pretty common sense to me and the officer I am defending is somehow wildly off-base to the plaintiff and his or her "expert." I once defended a constable whom a suspect tried to run over three times before the constable finally opened fire on the fellow only to find himself in court with an expert saying he should have "just run away!" Just run away, eh? We won the case, but I must say, between depositions and cross-examinations being an expert witness is one bizarre experience.

To further prove my point I must go back to my very first awareness of "expertness" that occurred decades ago when JW cited a miscreant who had a rooster in her yard in Tucson. We had a strict ordinance against a "male fowl" being kept since roosters have an instinctual reflex to disturb the peace upon sunrise. You and I might laugh this off as just a simple fine and great dinner opportunity for the violator, but not so this outraged lover of Gallus domesticus, and JW soon found himself in Superior Court defending his citation.

It seems the Colonel's favorite dish has a tendency to be hermaphroditic every few thousand or so, and therein lay the appeal to the court. The rooster was actually a "hooster" or maybe a "ren," or so the appellant claimed. Picture the spellbinding moment in court when the judge sat stunned at this revelation, this "expert" claim of fact that rendered the citation void and the asexual fowl legal!

Without hesitation our young crime fighter took the stand and declared that while true one might find a hermaphroditic chicken, he had checked the violating bird and found him wholly male . . . period. Thus began a long query by the judge regarding JW's vitae as a "chicken expert." Incredibly, his life as a Wyoming rancher included a great deal of chicken ranching and state fair judging that had led him into the world of chicken-checking!

And so JW became the official chicken checker of Tucson PD . . . a cross he bears to this day. I still laugh at the comments our dispatchers and officers came up with every time a "crowing rooster" call would go out when our squad was working the streets!

I know this all sounds rather strange, but to tell the truth, in my experience as an expert witness the tale of the chicken-checking expert is one of the less bizarre. As you laugh to yourself and get ready to go on your shift, know that for everything you do there is an expert somewhere who is willing to say you are wrong. On the other hand, there is also an expert willing to say, "Good job."

THE MARATHON

Train realistically and know your limits.

Once upon a time I fancied myself quite the runner. I would read my Runner's World, set new sights on running mileage, and think of the next race I would run. I was living in Teec Nos Pos on the Reservation and had a really cool six-mile course that meandered up through the oil rigs and ended in an exhilarating downhill dash down Teec Mountain in northern Arizona.

Even though I weighed around 190, I had the odd illusion that I was a potential greyhound instead of the plodding Clydesdale I really was. One afternoon I was sitting in the Port of Entry talking to my childhood friend and fellow DPS officer Gonzo when he said we should run the Fiesta Bowl Marathon in December. "Absolutely!" was my affirmation. And so my training began in earnest with daily six-mile runs on a nice soft dirt road that led from my house trailer to the mountain that lay behind.

Teec Nos Pos was the perfect location to establish a training lifestyle back in 1979. We had no television reception and only one FM radio channel, so the normal modern distractions were not present. I read, trained, tried being a vegetarian, and patrolled the remote roadways of the Navajo Reservation still under the odd illusion I was meant to be a runner. It was an interesting time in my life and I wouldn't have missed it for the world, although I think I could have done without the marathon . . .

December 1st found Gonzo and me pounding on the hard pavement of the roadway between Cave Creek and Scottsdale amid several thousand other folks desperately trying to reach the finish line at the Scottsdale Community College. Soon I began to fully realize how important it was to train on the same surface you were going to race on. My calves screamed, my feet ached, my shoulders hurt, and my damn nipples were burning! You didn't see that coming did you?

As we struggled around the 15-mile mark an elderly woman passed us rather crisply and we were aghast to read the back of her shirt: "I'm 65 and a grandmother, but I'm ahead of YOU!" We were outraged, and if only we could have caught up to her we would have given her a piece of our minds.

At the 21-mile mark Gonzo was cramping so badly he stopped to stretch out and I knew if I stopped I would surely stay stopped. At the 23-mile rest stop I sat for a minute to drink and rub my burning left knee, which was swollen like a melon. "The first-aid vehicle will be here in a minute!" a concerned voice behind me shouted, and I saw one of the race attendants staring at my knee. Mumbling something about having come this far I arose and stumbled on.

Four hours and 20 minutes after starting I stumbled across the finish line; Gonzo a moment later, still fighting horrible cramps, collapsed on the grass beside me. We both looked as if we had been in an extended interrogation with Jack Bauer. We compared training notes and realized we hadn't trained the way we should have for this re-enactment of Pheidippides' run from the Plains of Marathon to announce the Greek victory over the Persians; and then we remembered . . . that's what killed him!

I write this today as I get ready to head to the gym where I will ride a stationary bicycle and lift weights—training that matches my body type. Gonzo is a U.S. Marshal now and I am not sure if he runs anymore or not. Still, whenever we get together we laugh about that day so long ago when we learned once again the importance of training the way you are going to play, and that it's a darn good idea to know your limits.

MY LUCKY DAY

Sometimes a spate of bad luck can be the best thing that
happens to you.

—Death tugs at my ear and says: "Live, I am coming."

—Oliver Wendell Holmes, Sr.

Often we think that something that happens to us is a matter of bad luck,
yet it changes things so much that it becomes good luck! An example is the
day I was "killed."

It was my senior summer, and I was driving a tanker in the Coconino
National Forest looking for a small fire that one of the towers had picked
up following a thunderstorm. It was extremely rugged terrain, and we could
find no way to drive to the site of the fire.

Finally, one of our crew hiked in, found the burning tree on the side of
a steep canyon, and hiked a trail out to the roadway. When we got to the
fire, we found a huge tree shattered by lightning and burning from a point
about two-thirds of the way up. The fire could only be extinguished by felling
the tree. This would be no easy feat, as it leaned toward the slope making it
necessary to chop it down into the uphill side instead of the normally safer
way of dropping it on the downhill side.

I grabbed the Model 77 chainsaw and went to work with my buddy
John as my spotter holding my beltline and a crew from another tanker
standing off to the side to watch for any signs of danger. As I finished the
back-cut, the giant tree didn't fall over. Instead, it "sat" on my saw blade.
This is considered a very bad moment in the world of forestry and as a loud
thunderclap echoed up our canyon I looked up to my spotters to call for
wedges.

The thunder drowned out my call for wedges. It also drowned out the screams of my friends yelling, "RUN!" It seems the top third of the giant had burned through and was collapsing right this moment toward the bottom of the tree where I stood trying to cut it down. Thank God for our innate ability to read terrified body language, as I immediately recognized the contorted faces as screams. Adrenaline coursed through me, and I turned to race away.

Unluckily, I stepped out into space. The hill I was on was so steep that my initial leap carried me about 20 feet face first right into the ground, spraining both my wrists when I used them to break my descent. I turned to find the massive chunk of burning tree only yards away hurtling toward me. There was no escape; I was dead for sure.

Then, the most complete calm came over my conscious mind. I mean deep peace. I can't explain it; I can only tell you it was a complete release of my conscious self. Fortunately, my primitive "lizard brain" wasn't going so quietly.

I literally kicked the tree as it came down on me and that rolled me out from under it. Luckily, my helmet stayed on and my head was on the downhill side because a large limb hit me in the back of the head, burying my face into the thick pine needle cushion under me and knocking me sillier than a three-year-old at a Chuck E. Cheese's.

Everyone who witnessed this thought I had just been crushed to death. But my kick saved me, and the burning embers under me brought me to my senses. I rose from the smoke and stumbled out to the amazement of my cohorts.

I am the first to say that it's terribly bad luck to have a large tree fall on you. But believe me, it's incredibly good luck to have been so close to death and survive. For me, perhaps this was my luckiest day, as it changed my path in life. I went back to college and began to look for a way to live life as an adventure. Three weeks after college graduation I was in the police academy. And, yes, I got my adventure. How lucky can one guy be?

WHERE DID JOHN WAYNE GO?

The great American hero is still alive and well and in uniform.

"God grants liberty to those who love it and are always ready to guard and defend it!"

—Daniel Webster

John Wayne was the hero of my youth. He won World War II, tamed the Wild West, and generally went through life kicking butt. We hardly even remembered or cared about the name of any of the characters he played; we just went to a John Wayne Movie . . . period, enough said.

Then in the late 1960s, movies began to change. The anti-war movement, anti-West academia, and anti-authoritarian philosophy reshaped the image of the American hero to the anti-hero who stood against "The Man." By the time I graduated from college and became "The Man," law enforcement and almost all the warrior images of our culture had been denigrated to the point of derision by the elites.

No longer did the true hero fight for the American way; he or she exposed the evil "Military-Industrial Complex." No longer did the hero put on a uniform and fight crime. In fact, in most movies of the 1970s, the uniformed police officer became the symbol of oppression. I can remember driving proudly by my Alma Mater, The People's University of Arizona, on my way to my beat as a rookie and having former classmates oinking loudly at the faceless oppressor of the people driving by on his way to suppress somebody's rights somewhere.

Since I had minored in sociology to keep my grade point up, I decided to study the social phenomena leading to the loss of the heroic image. I have never found the answers to all my questions as to why free societies entertain the very beliefs that eventually will destroy their essential freedoms, but if you study history you find democracies tend to do this. That's why we were founded as a republic, not a democracy.

But every once in a while, the American people get a reminder of what's at stake in the world. For this generation, it was the 9/11 attacks. Since that day, there's been a real rebirth of the traditional view of the hero in American popular culture. The epitome of this new American hero is Jack Bauer on the hit TV show "24." This fellow kills bad guys without remorse, laments the loss of his heroic friends, and generally foils plots to destroy us.

You have to suspend disbelief while watching "24." Nobody could survive a single hour of Jack Bauer's adventures, much less a full 24-hour day of them. But the show is damn fun entertainment and one hell of an interesting morality play. On "24," good is good, bad is bad. There is no relativism, no anti-hero, no anti-establishment, no "we are the cause of our own enemies" malarkey. This is good old-fashioned Western-style justice being meted out by this generation's stoic warrior.

Ultimately, I believe it's important that our popular culture promote the image of the American warrior as a hero. Our fate as a free people depends on heroes: the warriors, soldiers, sailors, Marines, airmen, and cops like you. The challenge of today is to keep faith in our mission of freedom and not surrender to the coming storm of animosity toward the heroes who serve and protect.

John Wayne is long dead and whatever happens to Jack Bauer, "24" is just a television show. In the real world today, in Afghanistan, Iraq, and here in America, warriors pick up their weapons and go on a mission. Before you go on yours, take a moment to look in the mirror and see a real hero.

YOU BET YOUR BADGE

Once you become a cop, there are higher stakes for what you say and do.

One of the strangest things we do in our crime fighting career is play a game I like to call, "You Bet Your Badge." Just graduating from the academy and having the thrill of that badge being pinned to your chest instantly enters you in the game where things you do and say can cause that wonderfully important piece of metal to be removed.

The first time I played it intentionally I was a rookie racing to a "complainant fighting with a burglar in his home" call. I was flying and suddenly realized I couldn't make the light before it turned red so I stomped the accelerator, flipped on my lights and siren, and busted the red light at Mach 1. What a rush! This is called the "action phase" of the game.

It also turned out to be a rush for Lt. Ronstadt, who was sitting in the first row of cars at the same intersection about to go on a green light in his unmarked vehicle when a brilliant flash of lights and screaming siren exploded into the intersection on his left and raced past him into the night.

Other officers "Code 4'd" us, calling us off, so I went back to my beat blissfully ignorant I was into a round of YBYB.

Step two of the game is usually done by writing a report or sitting down with someone who initiates the "administrative phase" or the "spin the wheel phase" of YBYB. In this case, I found myself waiting outside the watch commander's office after an odd phone call in which I was asked if I had been driving vehicle 93 the night before. Good, then I better get "my butt" into Ronstadt's office after briefing.

Walking from roll call to the office, one of the old timers grabbed me in the stairwell. "Listen, Smith, whatever you did last night is done and the L.T. is a straight shooter if you are, so don't go in there and spread a bunch of BS; tell him what happened and why, especially why!"

And so it came to pass I was summoned before the L.T. and he asked me why I had tried to kill him and other citizens of the fine City of Tucson. What, perchance, was I thinking?

So I told him what I was thinking, why I was racing to help, why I felt I could safely bust the light since it seemed so close, and that I was sorry for taking years of life from him in that fashion. I confessed, and as I did the red seemed to drain from his face and his breathing became more relaxed and not so much like a great bellows heating the fires of Hell.

So began the final phase of our game, the "and the wheel stops on" phase. The lieutenant said in a cool but not mean voice, "This is between us, Smith, it stops here. But this is your one-time freebie; you will never do this again. Do you understand?" As I was the model of understanding, he told me to leave. As I got up he said almost under his breath, "If you hadn't done that last night you would never have been worth a damn as a cop, but don't do it again!" He did this while writing something and only looked up as he said the last four words.

That was 1975 and to this day I remember both lessons from my first round of "You Bet Your Badge." First, every decision you make may affect your career and whole life; that is the nature of our profession. I have seen guys ruin their careers with very poor decisions. It was their choice and they knew they were contestants when they made their decisions. But, it is usually not just the decision in the "action phase" that kills their future. It's trying to change what is already done by lying or misleading or hiding the truth. That old timer was right on those stairs so long ago, so remember to avoid the "BS."

BAD HABITS

Employing lazy tactics on the job can get you hurt, or worse.
Curious things, habits. People themselves never knew they
had them.

—Agatha Christie

I have always loved the above quote, partly because I have had so many bad habits pointed out to me during my life. It is funny that habits are so invisible to those of us who have them, which would be all of us. And most habits can be divided into the categories of good and bad.

Good habits, like flossing regularly, are usually pretty hard to develop. Bad habits seem to just appear or have been programmed into our brain by some sinister force that comes in our sleep and encodes our finger to sneak into our nose to snag that nasty little booger even when folks are looking.

I am constantly saying it is one of the primary jobs of supervisors to look for bad habits in our folks and point them out when discovered. We all know that many of our habits can get us hurt if they are done at the wrong time or reduce our ability to respond to a sudden assault or any other critical event that might occur. My wife, the Sergeant, has taken this concept so seriously she is constantly pointing out my bad habits, even in public.

I've explained at length that I can quickly retract my finger to defend myself if necessary and I am not even on the job anymore and besides, I am running around with an armed Sergeant for a wife. This disclaimer never seems to bring relief from her direct supervision of my bad habits.

OK, quit laughing. Because now it is time to get to your bad habits. I am not talking about your nose-picking, mustache twirling, throat clearing, or ear drilling bad habits. I am talking about your habits that you probably haven't paid attention to in years and are exactly the ones we see when we are reviewing an officer-involved injury, accident, or shooting. We see all sorts of things pop up that can only be explained as bad habits the officer, deputy, or trooper has developed in his or her time on the job.

How many times have you seen a video of an officer getting assaulted with hands in pockets just prior to the attack, turning his back on the subject when using the radio, or standing next to a violator reading the implied consent law within easy striking distance?

How often do you do these types of things? Hopefully you have a sergeant or a supervisor who points these dangerous habits out when you do them, but usually we don't. This is one of those "look in the mirror" moments when you need to really self-evaluate.

The truth is the vast majority of people we deal with are "yes" people who only want to get their darn ticket and get home. Every time someone tries to kick our butts and we have him fully subdued and cuffed and searched we should look deeply into his eyes and say, "Thanks, I needed that!"

These are folks who break our bad habits by reminding us we need our hands out of our pockets and ready to react quickly to a strike, that we never turn our back on subjects, and we keep our bodies bladed to anyone we are talking to. These good habits often get replaced by bad habits and we need to get that fixed!

If you are lucky enough to have a camera in your vehicle use it to monitor yourself, kind of like going over the game film after a ballgame. How do you stand? Where do you stand? What little habits do you have: good and bad? I know this seems odd but the longer it's been since someone tried to hurt you, the worse your habits may have become, so look at this as a kind of mental check-up.

If you are really, really lucky you're married to a sergeant who monitors your bad habits and corrects them as soon as you do them since the sooner you receive feedback the better the learning.

"What's that, Honey? No, I . . . I put the lid down . . . honest."

HAIL-FELLOW-WELL-MET

Some people are just born to be leaders and great cops; I've
been lucky enough to know one.

My motorist assist wasn't going very well. What had looked like a standard
assist with two fellows having a problem towing a vehicle had turned
"hinky."

Their answers just didn't ring true, and they kept trying to get me in
between them.

Backing out and telling them I was letting them handle their problem
after I threw out a couple of flares, I got back to the radio and called for a
backup ASAP.

Radio advised the plates had come back "negative" and a tac unit was
en route. I breathed a sigh of relief and, as I exited my vehicle, my backup
was already pulling up.

The door of the unmarked unit swung open and a giant of a man pulled
himself out of the car. Fran Karn was no stranger to this rookie. He had
been my PT and DT instructor in the academy, and even though he had
tried to be the "drill instructor" type his humor and informal leadership
skills made him not only our favorite instructor, but the one who we all
hoped to become.

Everything Fran did, he did well. When he left the academy, he went
right into Tucson's tactical unit, which worked special assignments and
surveillances as well as acted as assisted patrol with any major arrest or
crime.

So this night Fran walked by me watching the suspicious vehicle and
subjects as I began talking about how weird these two dudes were acting.
Without taking his eyes off the vehicles and subjects, he walked to the rear
of the towed vehicle, reached down to the license plate, and picked it up.

It wasn't even attached and worse, it was a front plate covered with bugs! "Yep," he said, "I'd call this suspicious."

After the two suspects confessed to stealing the towed vehicle from a repair shop and were sent off to the county in a transport unit, Fran patiently explained the signs of a stolen vehicle. He never criticized me, he only encouraged me.

A couple of years later I was sitting with Fran in a tac car, and we were doing surveillance. I must confess I had chosen that path because it was one Fran had chosen.

Eventually, we both went our separate ways. Fran went to a special anti-drug organization and I went to work for the Arizona DPS. I assumed our paths would only pass again by coincidence. In early 1987, I was given a marvelous squad of agents in the Southern Region based in Tucson. Much to my delight Fran Karn had been brought into our unit.

Again, it was my turn to marvel at this man who never took a sergeant's test, but ran every unit he was ever in with natural informal leadership abilities. I was the Sergeant, but he was "The Man."

Fran loved police work and cared for everyone he worked with. He was and is the best cop I ever knew. He always reminded everyone of officer safety and was always willing to be "the key" on any locked door we came upon in a warrant entry. His great mass turned many a door into matchsticks, but it was his unhesitating courage that really led us into harm's way.

If you are truly lucky you will have someone like this in your department, man or woman, you automatically think of when someone says, "a hail-fellow-well-met."

He called my house just the other day. He is retired now and living with his wonderful wife in Yuma, so he can spend his days with his grandkids. We laughed over old times and good friends and when we hung up I thought how lucky I had been to have a man like him in my life, one that I tried to model the best I could.

TO DELAY IS HUMAN

Why do today what you can put off 'til tomorrow?

One of the things that really drives me crazy is when someone procrastinates. I just don't understand why some people put off critical tasks until the last possible minute. I know my editors are sitting at their desks shaking their heads in wonder and alternately laughing and cursing at my apparent hypocrisy, but I must protest that they simply don't understand how I use deadlines as special "intensifiers" to my mental processes.

In fact, many a commander was amazed at how my evaluations would appear only at the appointed hours at which I would become essentially a police pumpkin rather than a sergeant.

My wife, the Sergeant, is constantly calling me a procrastinator, but I just don't think she gets my logic. For instance, she was commenting on my piles of camouflage clothing as being in her way as she tried to walk around our home office.

"My God!" she cried, "the hunting season has been over for months!"

"That's right," I calmly replied with my powerful command presence honed over my years of crime fighting and teaching young cops. "And that means the next season is just a few months away, so I might as well just keep them here."

After putting my camo clothes away in the attic, I began to reflect on the years of accusations I had faced, and the common term thrown at me . . . procrastinator. I thus resolved to study this misunderstanding.

When one studies the nature of procrastination, it becomes immediately apparent that it is one of the most common of human traits. In fact, it might be said the folks who jump right on things and get them done immediately are the deviants. When C. Northcote Parkinson wrote his famous law, "Work expands to fill the time allotted," he was simply explaining that it is a natural human trait to take as much time as possible to get things done.

Jane Burka and Lenora Yuen in their book, Procrastination, wrote that the primary reasons for this tendency are a fear of failure, a fear of success, a need to control, and a need to be perfect . . . hmmm. It seems each of these has a cost and procrastination is one way to pay the bill.

There appear to be a multitude of reasons why we put things off, but the real issue is: what is the effect of waiting to get those evaluations done 10 minutes before the lieutenant calls you to tell you that you will soon have the only walking beat in the Highway Patrol!?

Procrastinating can take a terrible toll on us if we let it get out of hand. And a lot of officers do. It can hurt you professionally and personally and, even though it is an acknowledged human trait, it is one we need to fight since the greatest toll is to the procrastinators themselves. Doing things late or not at all is a sure way of creating a huge amount of stress within.

In the crime-fighting profession, procrastination can also get us hurt or killed. For example, after you qualify, your firearm needs to get cleaned now, not next week, or even next year for some of you.

I suggest you start fighting your procrastinating tendencies by picking a single goal at a time and getting it done right now. In other words, change your habits to the unnatural state of doing things promptly. I know this sounds crazy, but it is important and most of you reading this have something you need to have done already but have put off.

Even I have things I have put off that need to get done . . . like my next chapter since this one is a bit tardy . . . and then there's the thank you cards from my last birthday, no . . . not my last . . . my fiftieth, and of course there's the . . .

CUTTING THROUGH THE NOISE

Truly important information often gets lost in today's barrage
of high-tech transmissions.

I just got done updating my Facebook page. Before I update my MySpace page I thought I better get this chapter out to the editors before I get one of those nasty little IMs about procrastinating. I'm not procrastinating, I'm communicating. What a day and age, when my Blackberry is vibrating and my computer is "pinging" and just a few days ago the phone on my wall actually rang. Those crazy old landlines still work, God bless them.

The thing is that just because we have an exponential growth in the ability to communicate with each other doesn't mean we actually have more things to say to each other. In fact, I find the world is filled with more and more "noise" that makes it difficult to find the actual "signal" that is the information we truly need. I have a satellite television signal that gives me channel upon channel of "noise" and very little actual stuff I want to watch, much less get any real information from.

Honestly, when I look at the cockpit of the modern police vehicle I am dazzled by all the great electronics so many of them have today. I happen to think a lot of this actually causes so many distractions it injures or kills more than a few crime fighters every year . . . but I am still dazzled.

Not to sound too much like an old geezer, but I remember back when we didn't have MDCs or MDTs or cell phones or smart phones or even portable radios. You got out of your car and you better have as much information as you could get from your dispatcher, call-taker, or whoever could tell you what you might be getting into where you were going; once you stepped out of that vehicle you were in the "wilderness" compared to today's GPS-filled high communication universe.

For us, it doesn't matter where the important "signal" comes from, just that we attend to it. I remember responding to an alarm way up on the north side of my beat on a graveyard shift when we were having a rash of smash and grabs, and I wanted to get there ASAP. I was just off probation and only slightly cocky, so I decided to go "on scene" before my backups arrived. JW, Sam, and Charlie were busting their butts trying to get there but I suavely advised Barb, our dispatcher, I was going "23" anyway.

"Be advised, 31 is only two minutes away," an icy voice replied. "I am '23' to the Southwest quadrant," I jauntily replied. Sam took the other quad in a few seconds and Charlie and JW arrived and cleared the perimeter in what turned out to be a false alarm.

It was a busy night and everyone cleared quickly and I finished up the paperwork as Barb's voice cut the air: "Three Adam Thirty-Two, check out at a Twenty-One." I thought, "Funny how a simple tone of voice can contain tons of information in it" . . . not ha-ha funny, but that "oh no" kind of funny.

In those days there was a strange item known as a "pay phone" and you kept the numbers of all the ones in your beat so you could simply pull up to one, tell dispatch the number, and answer the phone when it rang. Which is exactly what I did then, as quickly as possible, to allow Barb to give me a signal. It was a no noise message, very clear . . . if I ever disregarded her hint about waiting for backup again I would be eligible to sing for the Vienna Boy's Choir without difficulty. Pure signal, no noise.

I sometimes think back to those days of vastly limited communication and wonder if we get lax about sending such important messages because we are so inundated with information today. Barb's simple signal changed my behavior and maybe saved my life. You don't get many more important messages than that, and I hope you all take the time to listen carefully through all the noise, to get the right messages. Got to run. My "Twitter" needs updating.

THE GREATEST HAPPINESS

Victor Hugo wrote that "life's greatest happiness is to be loved."
He was absolutely right.

The other day I stopped by one of those coffee shop/bookstore places on the way to do an interview. The long flight and four-hour drive the day before had left my knees and back stiff and sore.

Looking around the bookstore I noticed there were hundreds of books on how to be happy. I thought about how the great psychologist Abraham Maslow argued that we were a whole species of gripers.

I have to admit that I was griping that morning. I tried a little French roast, and it sort of spoiled an otherwise happy experience. And the rental car was OK, but the seats weren't the most comfortable.

My gripes would soon disappear.

Carrie, the wife of the officer I came to interview, met me at the door and told me that her husband Mike needed to go to physical therapy by 10:30.

Mike needs therapy because he was shot in the head in 2004, and suffered massive injuries. In the interview, he described how the shooting went down. He described how it felt to come out of a coma and go through uncounted surgeries, and how he found such joy as little things he used to be able to do began coming back to him. For example, he described how happy it made him to be able to feed himself.

Three years after the shooting, Mike is still in pain. But he says he welcomes it as proof he isn't paralyzed.

Mike used to be a 187-pound jock; now he has a withered right arm and can barely walk. He says it was a good thing the bullet hit him and not someone who couldn't have survived it. Mike is so determined to be strong again that he lifts weights three times a week to supplement his physical therapy.

Yeah, Mike is strong. But Carrie is even stronger. Mike told me the greatest thing in his life is his wife, who has given up so much for him; his eyes fill with tears. At that point, my eyes watered as well. Allergies.

Next I interviewed Carrie, who described the horror of having the love of her life shot, of being told he wouldn't survive and that he would be a vegetable even if he did. She didn't believe it and talked to him constantly when he was in a coma and, when he came out of it, she began moving his limbs so he could walk someday. She was told he would be a quad. But Mike constantly complained of the pain. And she knew that where there is pain there is hope.

During our conversation, Carrie talked of all the officers who helped her keep her family together as they were moved from specialty hospital to specialty hospital. The officers always made sure there was someone there; one even made Carrie eat when she refused to leave her wounded warrior's side.

Mike sat to my left, silently weeping as his wife told of her incredible struggle to get everyone to believe in Mike and get him walking and talking, and all I heard in her voice was her pride in him and love for him.

Throughout the interview they joked and laughed; they laughed a lot . . . they are happy. And later, as I was packing up, I accidentally walked in on these two heroes holding each other, her head was on his shoulder; they smiled at me, a little embarrassed, but they didn't let go.

I turned away a little embarrassed myself, but I noticed my knees and back didn't hurt so bad. My life was a wonder of family and friends, and I was happy too. Except my allergies were really getting to my eyes right about then.